Poems of The Destined Lovers

Ivy Row

BookLeaf Publishing

Poems of The Destined Lovers

Presentation by *BookLeaf Publishing*

Web: www.bookleafpub.com

E-mail: info@bookleafpub.com

ISBN: 9789357443241

First edition 2023

O

Your lies, so beautifully composed.
Consumed by the idea of love, I let my guard down and welcomed your lies like flowers.

S

My anxiety screams run away from him,
run as fast as you can.
but stay forever

J

Silly boy, you're comedically beautiful.
Nonstop laughter fills our nights

N

At first you were a mistake
A mistake so effortlessly welcomed
A mistake beautifully orchestrated by the
universe

S

Oh my dear lover boy,
I pray that you heal from the pain
that torments you.

A

24 hours in
Sin City
With
You

J

I knew from the start you were not my forever, but what we created were the most beautiful blessings of this lifetime.

O

I'm offering all my love to you,
but you refuse me.
You tell me I'm not like the others,
that I'm special,
but yet you hide me in the shadows of your heart.

N

I can't deny the connection. I want you,
but I also can't deny the red flags.

S

He was the biggest misfortune of my life.

A

Once I saw you,
my soul can never unsee you

O

Night after night you left me crying in our bed,
Begging you not to leave me for her.
Asking what I can do to make you stay.
I would do anything,
Anything, please stay.
Abandoning my dignity for love so poisoned
For love that never belonged to me

A

He was the symphony to all my senses.
creating the sweetest love melody playing
through my being.

O

You were literally the ugliest person on this
planet,
but my love for you made you beautiful.

A

Your foreign language speaks
Magic to my soul,
yet at the same time
brings sorrow to my heart
knowing you're at a distance from my love.

S

He was the dark entity in my life,
Forever plaguing my soul.

J

How can I trust you,
let alone spend my life with you,
When your cloud of judgement
poisons my love
for you.

S

Arrogant son of a bitch, Please heal yourself.

N

And just like that, our atmosphere changed.
What was once magic
left me in complete despair.

A

I never believed in love at first sight.
Until you came along & flipped my entire
universe upside down.
Right there under a warm starry night
I fell blindly in love with you.

N

I was not interested,
was never about it
& look at me now.
Consumed with unrequited emotions

S.A

Mi estrella brillante
Dese la noche que te conocí
Endulzaste mi vida
mil porcento.

J

Please forgive me my love,
the universe has invited
me in a different direction
apart from you.

S.A

He was the angel I asked the universe
I needed at this moment in my life.
The star player of my dreams

M

The boy in art class that painted my first heartbreak.

My love language has always
been you

A

Our
chemistry
was
out
of
this
world.

So unexplainably cosmic

S.A

Amor mío, no se que vaya a ser de nosotros, pero este tiempo contigo sé que fue destinado por el universo.

A

Oceans apart,
I can still hear the sound of your voice so
perfectly.
It lingers like sweet music to my ears.
The melody that stays on repeat.

Future Soulmate

Come mine, for this love will last a lifetime.

future soulmate

I long for your touch,
I yearn for your presence
to lay my eyes on you is
life’s biggest present

www.ingramcontent.com/pod-product-compliance
Lightning Source LLC
Chambersburg PA
CBHW051754130826
49812CB00033B/1154
9789357443241